THE A4 PACIFICS

P. N. TOWNEND

LONDON
IAN ALLAN LTD

Previous page:
No 60010 *Dominion of Canada* is passing Perth shed as a 'J38', No 65929, prepares to leave light engine in June 1964. This was one of five 'A4s' remaining on the Eastern Region after the closure of Top Shed and they had a few more years' service working over the former Caledonian main line between Glasgow and Aberdeen on the sharply timed three-hour expresses.
K. R. Pirt/Colour Rail SC532

First published 1989

ISBN 0 7110 1813 8

© Ian Allan Ltd 1989

Published by Ian Allan Ltd, Shepperton, Surrey; and printed by Butler & Tanner Ltd, Frome and London

PREFACE

The introduction of the streamlined locomotive *Silver Link* in 1935 created a sensation in the national press and with the general public that has not been equalled by the construction of any other new railway engine in this century.

Probably many of the spectators who flocked to see the new locomotive, and undoubtedly some of the staff of the LNER, questioned the wisdom of having the hitherto handsome Gresley Pacifics encased in this way, but the carefully considered design has stood the test of time and the streamlined shape was retained throughout the working life of the class.

No other engine has created the impression of speed more than the Gresley 'A4' Pacific, both by its appearance and by a performance unmatched in this country for a new locomotive. *Silver Link* shattered all previous speed records on its inaugural run with the press on board the new 'Silver Jubilee' train within a few days of construction. The average speed of 100mph for 43 miles has never been equalled with steam traction in Britain, although such running has been surpassed and is indeed commonplace 50 years later with modern forms of traction. The high speed train era began in 1935 with the introduction of the 'A4'. In July 1938 *Mallard*, built with a double Kylchap exhaust system, surpassed *Silver Link*'s record of 112·5mph and reached a peak of 126mph, setting a world record still not exceeded by a steam locomotive. The 'A4' was not the heaviest, longest or nominally the most powerful Pacific locomotive in the country but there have been few occasions when the maximum power produced by an 'A4' has been equalled.

Much attention was paid to the aesthetic appearance of the 'A4', the aerofoil and parabolic curves had to be just right, and the silver, grey and charcoal livery of the first four engines was carefully matched. It was however the garter blue with dark red wheels of the 'Coronation' 'A4s' which many will regard as the ideal livery for these engines. This was standardised for the class by the LNER, many locomotives also receiving chromium and bright metal finish to the lettering and other details. A long time after this livery had disappeared under BR standard green, the A4s were still known as 'blue uns' by the drivers at Top Shed. There is perhaps no finer sight today of a steam locomotive at work, running through the beautiful countryside of Britain than *Mallard* in garter blue with the valances over the driving wheels in situ and a light haze from its double chimney.

It is not surprising that few colour photographs exist of the 'A4s' in their prewar splendour but several are included in this volume. Colour photographs of moving and static locomotives really only became a possibility in the late 1950s, and the 1960s, in the period when the 'A4' locomotives ran with a double chimney. Most of the pictures in this volume date from this period. The balance has been redressed to some degree by including photographs of the preserved locomotives seen regularly at work on special trains over BR tracks in recent years. I am indeed grateful to all the photographers whose work has made this book possible and my special thanks are also due to Alan Butcher of Ian Allan Ltd who provided the slides from which I made this selection.

PRE-WAR

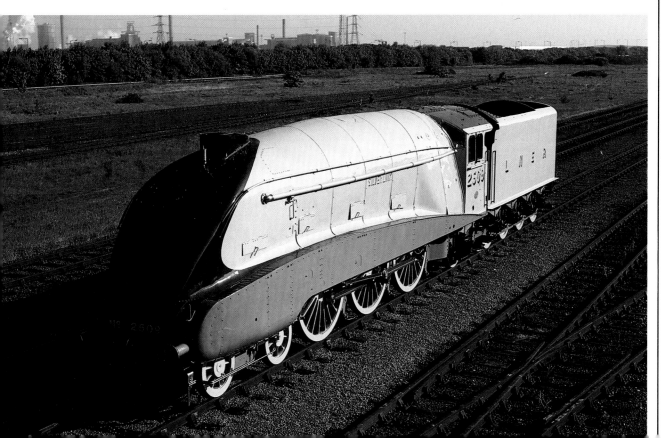

Front cover:
An up morning express, in the care of No 60019 *Bittern*, emerges from under St Leonard's Bank bridge, Perth, in 1965.
Richard Bromley

Left:
Cosmetically restored as No 2509 *Silver Link*, No 4464 *Bittern* displays the unique livery applied to the first four 'A4s'. The livery matched the 'Silver Jubilee' train and was in contrasting shades; the boiler casing, cab and tender sides were in silver grey, the valancing and frames in battleship grey and the front of the smokebox casing was painted charcoal. No lining out was applied and the names were painted on although nameplates had been manufactured for *Silver Link* and were fitted on the initial works trial runs. The restoration of '2509' was undertaken by the North Eastern Locomotive Preservation Group in association with an MSC scheme at ICI Chemicals & Polymers Ltd, Wilton.
Maurice Burns

Right:
No 4498 *Sir Nigel Gresley* is depicted in LNER garter blue livery standing in Darlington station at the head of an up express in August 1938. This, the hundredth Gresley Pacific to be built, was named after its designer who had been knighted for his work in 1936. No 4498 was unique at the time in having stainless steel edging to the bottom of the valances and tender sides but without the bright cut out numbers and letters fitted to the cabsides and tenders of the Coronation and West Riding 'A4s'. These details were added in 1939.
Colour Rail NE3

Above left:
Sea Eagle, **No 4487**, was one of a batch of 17 'A4s' ordered with government financial assistance in order to help reduce unemployment. It was built in 1937 and was one of five of this series to be painted in LNER green with a black smokebox. This gave an unsatisfactory appearance as there was a vertical edge to the black paint at the back of the smokebox instead of terminating at the sweeping curve at the front of the engine. These were the only 'A4s' with black smokeboxes until all received their wartime black livery, but their appearance was not marred for long, as early in 1938 *Sea Eagle* received the garter blue colour standardised for the class. The photograph was taken in July 1938 at Eastfield although it was a Haymarket engine at the time. The paint was about five months old, around halfway between shops repairs at this period, and shows how the dirt and staining occurred in certain areas although the top of the smokebox has not been cleaned at all.
J. P. Mullett/Colour Rail NE59

Below left:
No 4484 *Falcon* was another of the same series as No 4487 which also received a black smokebox with the green livery when new in February 1937. However by December of that year it was painted garter blue and is seen here the following August at Haymarket depot where it was allocated. It was usual for 'A4s' to stand on shed with the 'jaws open' for access to the smokebox in order to clean out the ash. When the engine was prepared for its next working the front would be closed by the fireman with a key which operated the winding mechanism, after checking the door inside had been fully tightened.
L. Hanson/Colour Rail NE40

Above right:

No 4482 *Golden Eagle* **was built at Doncaster in December 1936 and this photograph was taken soon afterwards. It was the first 'A4' built after the initial order of four for working the 'Silver Jubilee' and was intended for normal express service hauling teak stock. The locomotive was therefore painted in the standard LNER passenger green livery with the valancing black and green wheels. The green was carried slightly further forward than the silver grey used on the earlier engines or the garter blue used later. This left a narrower band of black where the handrail sweeps down at the front. Nine 'A4s' received the LNER green livery but only four were painted with the green carried forward in this way to the front. A corridor tender was fitted but this was secondhand, having been built in 1928 for the earlier series of non-streamlined Pacifics.**

G. Ford/Colour Rail NE58

Below right:

This slide is possibly the only one in existence showing No 4468 *Mallard* **on its record breaking day, 3 July 1938, when a world record speed of 126mph was attained. It is depicted on the down journey to Barkston where the train was turned for the return high speed run. Brake tests were carried out on the down journey at several points in order to test the new Westinghouse QSA (Quick Service Application) valves which permitted air to be admitted directly to each vacuum brake cylinder on the train. The dynamometer car can be seen behind the tender and a rake of Coronation twin coaches. The left hand injector appears to be giving trouble by the amount of steam escaping from the overflow pipe under the cab but this could not have been a problem on the return journey where both injectors would be required to maintain the prodigious steaming rate required.**

K. H. Leech/Colour Rail NE57

DETAILS

Left:
No 60011 *Empire of India* was one of five Coronation 'A4s' embellished with the coat of arms of the country the engine was named after. These were painted by hand at Doncaster Works onto metal plates which were screwed onto the cabsides. The works plates normally in this position were removed to the inside of the cab roof and on the Coronation 'A4s' these were chromium plated. When one of these engines arrived in the Plant works for overhaul it was the practice to remove the plates carrying the coat of arms immediately upon arrival so that they were not damaged as the engine was stripped down. The coats of arms were touched up as necessary and replaced on the locomotive after repainting. No 60011 carried the coat of arms to the end and was photographed at Ferryhill depot, Aberdeen, on 17 June 1962.
F. Hornby

Above:
**This unusual shot shows clearly the two apertures of the
Kylchap double chimney and the small holes to the rear for
ventilating the snifting or anti-vacuum valve, which was
usually positioned and visible behind the chimney on LNER
superheated locomotives. The valve was also situated on top
of the superheater header and allowed air to enter the
superheater elements when the regulator was closed. The
chimney casing was made of copper sheeting to prevent
corrosion and the chimney liners of cast iron machined to size.**
G. W. Morrison

Right:
**Twenty two of the 35 'A4s' constructed were fitted with
corridor tenders but the remainder were provided with a
streamlined non-corridor type first introduced in 1936. No
60003 *Andrew K. McCosh* seen here backing down at Kings
Cross station originally was fitted with the corridor type but
finally changed to the non-corridor pattern in 1955. The non-
corridor tenders were slightly narrower than the corridor ones
and were also slightly less in overall width than the cab. They
were not fitted with buck-eye couplers.**
G. Rixon

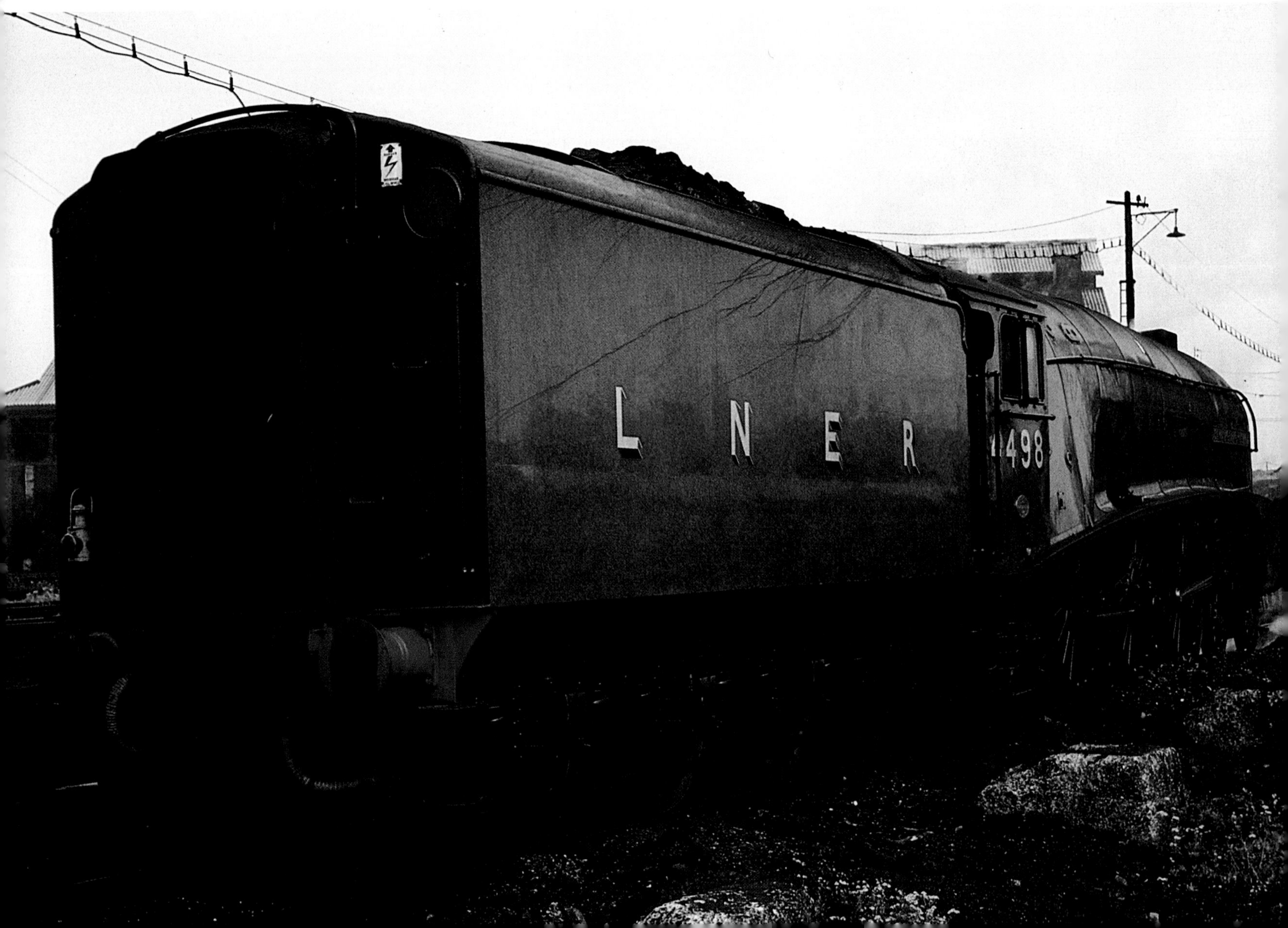
L N E R
498

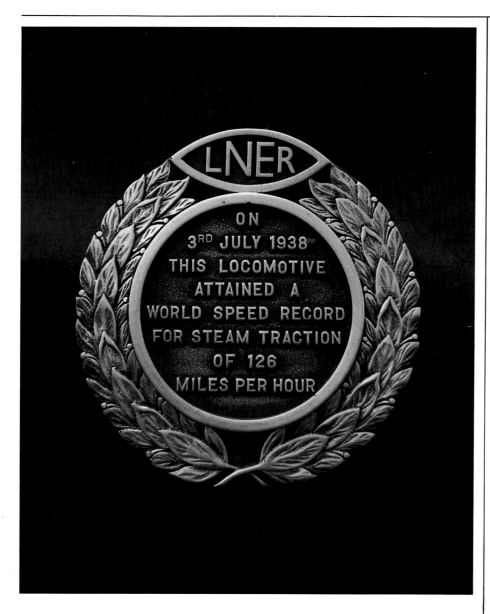

Far left:

Corridor tenders were first introduced by the LNER in 1928 and were fitted to the 'A1' and 'A3' class Pacifics for working the non-stop 'Flying Scotsman' between London and Edinburgh. The use of corridor tenders was necessary for a change of crew en route, one crew travelling half way in the train before changing over. No other railway used corridor tenders in normal service although the LMS built one, and the Union Pacific Railroad used the vestibule connections on the back of some of its tenders but with no corridor. The corridor tender seen here on the preserved 4498 *Sir Nigel Gresley* was one of the original batch of ten built in 1928 and slightly altered when fitted to the new No 4498 in 1937. The beading visible along the top was however retained and distinguishes the earlier tenders from the streamlined corridor type built new for the 'A4s'. *Sir Nigel Gresley* is seen here being prepared at Nine Elms depot prior to working a special train for the A4 Locomotive Society in June 1967.
G. Rixon

Left:

The plaques commemorating *Mallard's* record-breaking run in 1938 were not fitted to the engine until a 1948 overhaul at Doncaster works, by which time it had been renumbered E22. The omission of any commemoration of the run on the locomotive had been drawn to the attention of the LNER authorities from overseas and a photograph also requested had resulted in the Doncaster drawing office photographer being sent to Grantham only to find the engine in wartime black livery and in deplorable external condition with small numbers painted on the cab sides locally under the renumbering scheme. *Mallard* was the last 'A4' to retain its wartime livery but in 1948 it reverted to prewar garter blue for 18 months before receiving BR blue. Although the plaques state that 126mph was attained this speed was a peak which could only have been achieved over a few yards. The LNER and Gresley himself only claimed 125mph. The photograph was taken in March 1963 when the engine carried the BR standard green livery.
G. Rixon

Left:

A plaque was fitted to No 60009 *Union of South Africa* on the left hand side of the engine in 1954 at a Doncaster Works overhaul. This shows a springbok and was donated by a Bloemfontein newspaper proprietor. At the time the coats of arms were still fitted to the cabsides. These were removed before withdrawal, and since preservation in Scotland by John Cameron and his associates, the engine has acquired a further leaping springbok fitted to the cabside. The locomotive is seen here on the Ferryhill turntable after working a special train from Edinburgh in September 1979.
G. W. Morrison

Above:

One of the most famous locomotives of the steam era, *Silver Link* richly deserved to be preserved for its spectacular achievements in 1935, which introduced the high speed train era to this country. Sadly this was not to be and the nameplate shown here was still attached to the withdrawn locomotive some months after it was taken out of service in December 1962. When new in 1935, the original four locomotives built to work the 'Silver Jubilee' between Kings Cross and Newcastle ran in a silver grey livery with painted lettering on the boiler casing, although nameplates had been fitted on the works trial trips. These were removed before *Silver Link* entered service but nameplates were fitted again when the engine was painted garter blue in December 1937. The first two engines *Silver Link* and *Quicksilver* were given nameplates with rounded corners whereas all the other 'A4s' had square corners. Although cast in brass, the nameplates were originally chromium plated.
G. W. Morrison

Left:

Kingfisher **was built in December 1936 and unlike many of the other locomotives named after birds, it was retained until withdrawal in September 1966. Apart from a few months at Doncaster and Kings Cross, it had been allocated to Scotland for the whole of its working life but was photographed in March 1966 on a special Locomotive Club of Great Britain tour to Weymouth. The red background to the lettering was incorrect and should be black. The author, when Shedmaster at Kings Cross, preferred them red but was instructed to cease this local practice after correspondence from the Regional Chief Mechanical Engineer. This had arisen from a complaint by a photographer that the letters did not stand out clearly with a red background on the panchromatic black and white films generally in use at the time.**
G. S. Cocks

Above:

Four 'A4s' were painted in an experimental blue livery during the summer of 1948 in place of the LNER garter blue still in use until the following year. No 60028, which had only been renamed *Walter K. Whigham* **in 1947, ran the longest period in this experimental blue before receiving the then standard BR blue livery in the autumn of 1950. The engine was therefore painted in three different blues within a few years. The lining out in red, cream and grey was elaborately carried out in contrast to the LNER garter blue livery and unusually for the 'A4s' this followed the curved line of the footplating and down the casing ahead of the cylinders, terminating behind the buffers. It was photographed at Grantham depot in August 1948.**
J. M. Jarvis/Colour Rail BRE159

Above:
Mallard stands on the 70ft turntable at Doncaster depot on 17 June 1962. The large cylinder visible is the vacuum reservoir which enabled dead locomotives to be turned by means of the vacuum operated motor. The turntable at Doncaster Carr Loco shed had been removed before the last war and a turning triangle installed on a nearby marshy piece of land adjacent to the depot. Oddly this was removed after about 25 years and replaced by the turntable shown at the north end of the depot.
G. W. Morrison

Right:
Dominion of Canada is seen here in a typical shed scene at St Rollox, Glasgow, with the 'cod's mouth' open, on 31 March 1964, after working from Aberdeen. The idea of the wedge shape front was adopted from the Bugatti railcars used on the French railways, one of which can be seen in the railway museum at Mulhouse today. In the conditions laid down for the design of the streamlining of the 'A4' it was stipulated that the front should be capable of opening for access to the smokebox door and not foul any of the adjacent tracks. The horizontal wedge was ideal for fulfilling these conditions.
G. W. Morrison.

ENGINES ONLY

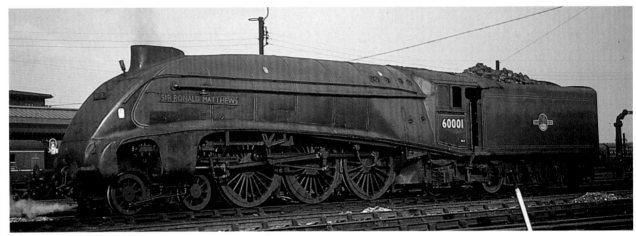

Above:
Gateshead Pacifics were not allocated to regular crews but nominated to particular workings, sometimes for very long periods. No 60001 was a Gateshead locomotive throughout its life and received number priority under the LNER renumbering scheme as it had been renamed *Sir Ronald Matthews* after the Chairman of the company a year after construction in March 1939. The previous chairman dropped to No 4! Perhaps there was something to be said for having the chairman of the LNER at the head of an East Coast express but the author personally preferred the bird names which were at least shorter. No 60001 is standing at Grantham. The up 'Flying Scotsman' was a regular Gateshead turn to Grantham where Top Shed men took over the train with their own 'A4' to Kings Cross. The Gateshead engine and crew took over the 3pm from Kings Cross at Grantham for their return working.
P. J. Hughes/Colour Rail BRE268

Right:
No 60017 *Silver Fox* was photographed in April 1962 at Doncaster depot although it was a Kings Cross engine from new until the depot closed in 1963. After a few months at New England the engine was withdrawn.
G. W. Morrison

Bittern, No 60019, stands on Perth depot on the 10 August 1965. It was allocated to Aberdeen Ferryhill and was withdrawn from service 13 months later. It was one of the last two to run on the Glasgow to Aberdeen route but for nearly all its working life **Bittern** had been a Gateshead engine.
G. W. Morrison

No 60019 **Bittern** was purchased after withdrawal from service in September 1966 by G. S. Drury, who arranged for it to be kept in the steam shed at York, now the National Railway Museum. It is seen here resplendent in BR green livery outside the depot in August 1968, before it was moved to Neville Hill shed at Leeds where it was repainted garter blue. After many years of storage out of use it has now returned to York where from the summer of 1988 it is on display in the guise of *Silver Link* at the National Railway Museum. It is now fitted with a single chimney with the valances restored and painted in the silver grey livery unique to the original four 'A4s' built for working the 'Silver Jubilee'.
Colour Rail BRE775

Left:
For much of its working life No 60023 *Golden Eagle* was a Newcastle engine, based at Gateshead and Heaton depots, but it is shown here at Haymarket in September 1961. Gateshead 'A4s' worked to Edinburgh daily from Newcastle. The engine was withdrawn in October 1964.
J. T. Inglis/Colour Rail SC536

Above:
A clean No 60032 stands outside the Mainline Running Shed at Kings Cross. *Gannet* was used the following day on the 'Elizabethan' to Edinburgh. Although the engine ran the lowest mileage of the class in over 25 years of service at 1,351,887 miles, this was nevertheless an average of over 53,000 miles each year. The double chimney was fitted for not quite the last five years of its life. The cost of fitting it in 1958 at just over £200 was certainly worthwhile in enabling the 'A4s' to achieve some spectacular performances and an everyday reliability working diesel diagrams to Newcastle and back in 12hr from King's Cross, turns not contemplated with steam traction in earlier years.
P. N. Townend

Left:

No 60005 was one of the last batch of 'A4s' built new in 1938 with the Kylchap double chimney as No 4901 *Capercaillee.* It was not named *Sir Charles Newton* after the Chief General Manager of the LNER until June 1943. The engine had been named after him during 1942 but new nameplates had to be cast after he was knighted. No 4901 was a very reliable and economical engine when new and worked from Gateshead until 1963. Unfortunately, as shown in this photograph taken at that depot in March 1963, the 'A4s' were not always kept clean. One Gateshead Pacific, usually very dirty, would work into Kings Cross daily with one of the overnight trains with its crew who lodged in London before returning with the 10.15pm 'Night Scotsman'. The engine was booked to stand at Kings Cross all day and it was usually prepared to stand pilot to cover the afternoon Top Shed turns to Newcastle. No 60020 was used on the 4.50pm 'Tees-Tyne Pullman' one
afternoon and as it was so dirty it was cleaned before departure. Within minutes of the train leaving the station there was a telephone call to the depot asking if the engine had been transferred to Kings Cross!
P. J. Hughes/Colour Rail BRE335

Above:

It was rare for the 'A4s' to work away from the former LNER East Coast main line but towards the end of steam operation, 'A4s' appeared at some unlikely depots. Here No 60011 *Empire of India* of Haymarket is seen on Holbeck shed after working the up 'Waverley' through from Edinburgh via Carlisle in place of a failed 'Peak' class diesel on 25 March 1962. The 'A4s' were not at that time seen regularly at work on either the Waverley or the Settle line.
G. W. Morrison

Above:
It fell to *Kingfisher*, No 60024, to head the last service train worked by an 'A4' locomotive on 14 September 1966 between Glasgow and Aberdeen, but the few remaining 'A4s' were in demand for special trains in many parts of the country. *Kingfisher* is seen here on the turntable at Nine Elms depot on the Southern Region, a long way from its usual base at one of the Scottish area depots. It was working a Locomotive Club of Great Britain tour to Weymouth on 27 March 1966.
G. S. Cocks

Right:
No 60007 *Sir Nigel Gresley* is awaiting overhaul at Crewe works and is seen at an Open Day on 4 August 1966, six months after withdrawal from British Railways, one of six to remain under preservation out of the 35 'A4s' constructed. It is standing next to the last Pacific design produced in this country, No 71000 *Duke of Gloucester*, also a three-cylinder engine and now preserved in working order. No 60007 has been stencilled on various parts of the lagging to aid identification when the locomotive was reassembled. The engine did not run again until the spring of 1967 when it attained 96mph within a few miles of leaving Crewe.
G. S. Cocks

AROUND KINGS CROSS STATION

Above:

No 60017 *Silver Fox* **arrives at Kings Cross from the North with a tender still fairly full of coal and had probably worked up from Peterborough or possibly from Cambridge if a bearing was being seasoned. The 'A4s' were very economical on coal and water as shown in the Interchange Trials of 1948 and this was the result of improvements in detail design by the technical staff at Doncaster with the earlier Pacifics. They were unsurpassed in this respect by any other Pacific locomotive in normal service in this country. The Brush diesel in the background is standing by the small tipper coaling plant in the station loco depot and the large square building above** *Silver Fox* **is the old Great Northern Railway warehouse in the Goods Yard which is contemporary with the station.**
G. Rixon

Right:

Mallard **was withdrawn from service in April 1963 and restored as far as practicable to its original condition for display in the British Transport Museum at Clapham the following year as part of the National Collection. It is seen here inside Kings Cross station about to leave Platform 10 on a short train on the 19 April, which must have been one of its last workings in regular service. The platform was No 10 to generations of steam enthusiasts although not originally so numbered and has now become No 8.**
G. Rixon

Left:

No 60025 *Falcon* is about to work the 6.20pm from Kings Cross to Leeds in May 1961. The tender is excessively coaled for this working which would be done by the crew going back for coal after the fire was made up on the shed. The running foreman would see the engine leaving the front of the shed, dropping down to the outlet signal and frequently without authority the crew would nip back on the inlet road to the coaling plant to top up the tender. This sometimes led to delays if the engine was then blocked in by incoming locomotives and to excessive amounts of coal on the tender which was trimmed off by the aqueduct inside the tunnel mouth at Kings Cross or fell off on the curve through Hatfield station, breaking the gates at the end of the platform.
B. Patton/Colour Rail

Above:

Union of South Africa, No 60009, has just been released from the 'Elizabethan' coaches at Kings Cross and is now waiting to cross over to the station loco depot where it will be coaled on the small tipper coaling plant. This was used so that the coal could be selected and any large lumps broken up before being put on the tender. Grade 1A coal, generally from Harworth or Rossington collieries was used. This coal could be very large and if a piece became jammed in the tender coal gate it could take the crew some time to break or move it. It was very hard coal, difficult to break in these circumstances but otherwise excellent for steaming 400 miles.
Colour Rail BRE8

Above:
***Quicksilver**, No 60015, is waiting to leave Kings Cross with a down express. The enclosed nature of the cab is apparent, with the flexible sheeting across the gap between the engine and tender. Later built Pacifics had the more usual space between the two which resulted in many complaints of draughts. One driver at Top Shed was a problem to the Shedmaster at Gateshead until the author advised him that the driver suffered with his back and if the Shedmaster were to take his 'A4' he must give him another even if rundown as he would not take an 'A1' because they were too draughty.
G. Rixon

IN SERVICE

Above:
The Scottish allocated 'A4s' were usually only seen working south of Newcastle in the summer months on the 'Elizabethan' to Kings Cross, unless visiting Doncaster Plant where the 'A4s' were maintained for most of their lives. Here No 60027 *Merlin* is seen heading south climbing to Stoke summit at Little Ponton on 5 September 1959. The headboard appears to be turned round the wrong way, which was usually done at weekends when the through engine working was maintained but not the nonstop run.
G. W. Morrison

Above:

Unusually No 60003 *Andrew K. McCosh* was photographed in March 1962 on the up 'Yorkshire Pullman' leaving Leeds at Beeston Junction, with a dark exhaust and some steam escaping around the front end. By the end of the year this Kings Cross locomotive had been withdrawn. This train was usually worked by Copley Hill 'A1' class engines and men, both working through to London. The crew returned the same day on another Copley Hill 'A1' having worked 372 miles, one of the longest daily turns in the country at the time.
G. W. Morrison

Left:
Kings Cross 'A4s' worked daily to Leeds Central station on the down 'White Rose' and 'Yorkshire Pullman' trains. No 60006 *Sir Ralph Wedgwood* is seen here blowing off at Leeds Central at the head of the 12.30pm express to Kings Cross on 6 March 1962.
G. W. Morrison

Above:
Silver Fox, No 60017, is making a clean start on an up express from Doncaster on a Sunday at 4.15pm, 29 April 1962, the clean maroon stock contrasting nicely with the green locomotive. The author remembers the Pacifics making starts from Doncaster in wartime on trains of over 20 coaches daily and had never witnessed such volcanic effects before from steam engines trying to start such loads. The track layout was the cause of much of the problem as the train would be out on the main line past the turn out and the end still beyond the turn in at the rear, precluding the use of the yard pilot at the back to give starting assistance.
G. W. Morrison

Right:
Union of South Africa, No 60009, was allocated to Haymarket from new in 1937 until 1962 when it was transferred after almost 25 years work to Aberdeen for the services to Glasgow. It is passing Perth shed on an up morning express to Glasgow Buchanan Street on 10 August 1965. These workings ceased the following year and 'No 9' was withdrawn for preservation in June 1966. The numbers of the 'A4s' were frequently abbreviated to 'No 9' or '22' in everyday parlance.
G. W. Morrison

Right:
Silver Link, **No 60014, is climbing out of Kings Cross, passing Holloway on a Leeds and Bradford express in August 1962. The engine is in clean condition with polished buffers and has the light exhaust of a double Kylchap locomotive, but despite its form the engine was withdrawn by the end of the year, having run over $1\frac{1}{2}$ million miles in 27 years of service on the East Coast main line, predominantly from Kings Cross depot but with two spells at Grantham.**
J. B. Snell/Colour Rail BRE773

Left:

The up 'Elizabethan' is leaving Edinburgh Waverley station at the start of its 392·7 miles nonstop run to Kings Cross in September 1961 headed by No 60022 *Mallard.* **This was one of the last runs of the celebrated train. These workings were first introduced in 1928 on an 8½hr timing but by 1961 this had been reduced to 6½hr.** *Mallard* **worked the last down run of the 'Elizabethan' from Kings Cross a day or two later. The working of this train had always been exemplary and it was rare for a locomotive to fail or lose any time over this long distance. The engines were invariably well cleaned with the motion and buffers brightly polished. It was truly the end of an epoch.**
J. T. Inglis/Colour Rail SC535

Above:
One of the hardest and most important trains worked by the Top Shed Pacifics was No 266 down, the Niddrie Goods, leaving Kings Cross Goods yard at different booked times over the years but at 3.05pm at one period. The turn was rostered to No 1 link and worked as a lodge turn to Newcastle by the regular men with their own nominated locomotive. A short break was taken at York whilst the coal was brought forward by a relief crew but it was nevertheless an arduous turn taking 7hr to Newcastle. The working was introduced specially to improve the working and punctuality. There was also the added incentive to arrive punctually as there was just time for well earned refreshment before closing time. The Kings Cross men excelled in fast running and No 266 down was no exception, but unfortunately not all the wagons arrived at their destination without being put off en route with hot boxes or parts falling off! The locomotive is No 60025 *Falcon*.
The late D. Cross

Right:
No 60017 *Silver Fox* was the first of the single chimney 'A4s' to receive a Kylchap double chimney in May 1957, although four of the class had been fitted with them when new in 1938. The engine is passing Hatfield on 30 July 1960 on a down express. The exhaust from the chimney is very wet which would suggest the engine was priming or had too high a level of water in the boiler at the time. Priming was not a problem at Kings Cross as all the water was softened and the introduction of polyamide after World War 2 had effectively prevented priming, enabling crews to run with higher levels of water in the boiler.
G. Rixon

Above:
Silver Fox is passing Ganwick on the up 'Tees-Tyne Pullman,' a Kings Cross lodge turn from Newcastle. Top Shed drivers Graham and Tee had this engine regularly for some time and like most of the crews in this link performed their work in an exemplary fashion.
The late D. Cross

Right:
No 60025 *Falcon* is waiting to leave Leeds Central station with the up 'White Rose', which was the last regular steam working from Leeds to Kings Cross when photographed on the 15 June 1963. A Pullman train can be seen in an adjoining platform. The headboard on the top lamp bracket carries the white rose of Yorkshire emblems. The author had the task of designing one or two of these decorative emblems for other headboards and it was a disappointment afterwards to find that many of them went missing in general service.
G. W. Morrison

Left:
The down 'Grampian' express is just catching the low sun as it passes Dunblane headed by No 60031 *Golden Plover* which was always a Haymarket engine until reallocated to St Rollox in 1962 from where it worked a further 3½ years on the Aberdeen services. It was one of two 'A4s' surviving long enough to have the yellow stripe painted diagonally across the cab panels to indicate the engines were prohibited from working on the electrified lines south of Crewe. The photograph was taken in August 1965.
D. M. C. Hepburne-Scott/Colour Rail SC381

Above:
The up Car Carrier train is passing south of Retford hauled by No 60025 *Falcon* in June 1963, the month Top Shed closed. The engine did not survive long afterwards as it was withdrawn the following October from New England depot, where the surviving 'A4s' from Kings Cross had been transferred. A headboard had been provided for the Anglo-Scottish Car Carrier train a few years earlier when the train commenced running but it is not in use on this occasion.
P. Gater/Colour Rail BRE632

Above:
Well managed and designed steam locomotives did not need to emit dark smoke and on this June 1962 day No 60013 *Dominion of New Zealand* has a clean exhaust when passing York steam depot after starting away from the station on a down express.
G. W. Morrison

Right:
***Mallard* pauses for photographic purposes at Tiverton Junction on the former GWR West of England main line, whilst working a special train for the Locomotive Club of Great Britain from Waterloo to Exeter and back over the GWR route to Paddington on 24 February 1963, a few weeks before withdrawal and subsequent preservation. The 'A4s' had passed this way many years earlier in the Interchange Trials of 1948 in which the 'A4' had averaged the lowest coal and water consumption of any express engine tested, as well as achieving some outstanding performances over the severe gradients in Devon.**
G. W. Morrison

Above:

The verdant nature of Welwyn Garden City is not apparent on this photograph of No 60021 *Wild Swan* passing on an up express in April 1962, but at least the engine is in splendid form with plenty of coal left on the tender to reach Kings Cross.

T. B. Owen/Colour Rail BRE539

Right:

Although signalled to depart, No 60021 *Wild Swan* is standing quietly in Leeds Central station at the head of the blood and custard painted stock forming the 12.30pm express to Kings Cross on 23 March 1961, a scene once commonplace but which has now passed into history, as the station has long been closed and the facilities at Leeds concentrated at the City station.

G. W. Morrison

Above:

A spotless No 60004 is standing in Craigentinny sidings, Edinburgh, on an empty stock working. The background of the *William Whitelaw* nameplate has been painted in the Scottish regional blue which was used at stations throughout Scotland. The Eastern Region blue was much darker. It was not intended for nameplates but Haymarket depot painted the 'A4' nameplates locally in this light blue, as well as burnishing many of No 60004's components. The name replaced that of *Great Snipe* in July 1941 and was formerly carried by the first 'A1' class Pacific built by the North British Locomotive Co in 1924 before being transferred to an 'A4' after he had ceased to be chairman of the LNER.

J. T. Inglis/Colour Rail SC530

SINCE PRESERVATION

Left:
No 60009 *Union of South Africa* ran the highest mileage in service of any of the 'A4s', probably attaining over 1,800,000 miles by the time of its withdrawal in 1966. Before the end of steam the accountants had ceased to record steam locomotive mileages and the exact figure is not known, but *Union of South Africa* averaged some 62–63,000 miles per annum throughout its working life. The engine has retained its British Railways green livery since preservation and although based in Scotland has been seen regularly over BR, including south of the border, in recent years. It was photographed on the 'Forth and Tay' special leaving Dundee on the 7 June 1975.
G. W. Morrison

No 60009 *Union of South Africa* is passing through Princes St gardens Edinburgh on the 'Forth and Tay' special to Dundee returning via Perth on the 7 June 1975.
G. W. Morrison

The 'Cumbrian Mountain Express' hauled by No 60009 *Union of South Africa* is running southbound near Armathwaite on 31 March 1984. Initially under preservation this engine ran on the Lochty Private Railway in eastern Scotland and during the steam ban on British Railways it was the only 'A4' which could be enjoyed in steam. The engine has been seen at many steam events since the ban was lifted. It is turned out in exemplary condition, the BR green livery is the colour most people will remember the 'A4s' carrying when running in regular service.
R. Barnard

Right:

Mallard, No 4468, has been on static exhibition since withdrawal from BR, initially at the British Transport Museum at Clapham in South London, but latterly when that museum closed, at the National Railway Museum at York. The engine was restored to its original appearance at Doncaster Plant Works with the exception of some minor details. A non-corridor tender and valances over the wheels were refitted. Although the engine was not overhauled it was in good condition and it has been a comparatively straightforward task to restore it to working order in time for the 50th anniversary of its record-breaking run on the 3 July 1938. It is seen here under the splendid roof of York station on 26 April 1987.
J.C. Summerill

Far right:

Mallard is leaving York station with the '*Scarborough Flyer*' on 26 April 1987. Much of the cost of restoration was paid by the Scarborough Corporation who have done much to retain these popular excursions to their resort in recent years.
B. Robbins

Mallard newly restored to working order makes a splendid sight on 16 May 1987 appropriately working a 'Birdwatch Special' near Eldroth, sadly with few passengers for such a worthy locomotive.
L. A. Nixon

Sir Nigel Gresley is receiving attention at Carnforth shed. It is a very expensive business overhauling large steam locomotives, an operation which has to be carried out to BR standards and passed by their Inspectors if the locomotive is to run on BR track. For example, all the boiler tubes have to be removed every seven years for internal boiler examination.
H. Ballantyne

Left:
No 4498 *Sir Nigel Gresley* is maintained by members of the A4 Locomotive Society in excellent working order. The engine has worked regularly over BR since the ban on steam workings ceased in 1972. The garter blue livery has been restored but no attempt has been made to put the engine back into its original condition. The locomotive is hauling the 'Scarborough Flyer' on 2 May 1987, crossing the River Nidd at Knaresborough en route from York to Leeds.
W. A. Sharman

Above:
It was a pleasant change to see No 4498 *Sir Nigel Gresley* working a special train, passing Esher in June 1967 without a headboard fitted, but it does not help identification afterwards!
G. Rixon

Left:
Sir Nigel Gresley and the other 'A4s' preserved make
delightful photographs in scenic settings. The garter blue livery
is particularly attractive and here the low winter sun glints on
the streamlined casing of No 4498 whilst working a
southbound excursion near Armathwaite in November 1980.
L. A. Nixon

Above:
Sir Nigel Gresley has been a regular performer on the
'Cumbrian Coast Express' since returning to steam
operations over BR track. The restored cut out numbers and
letters stand out well in this photograph taken in 1978
crossing one of the river bridges on its return journey to
Carnforth.
W. A. Sharman

Left:
No 4498 *Sir Nigel Gresley* strides north at Bucknell near Bicester with the 'Nicholas Nickleby' on 25 January 1986.
W. A. Sharman

Above:
On 8 October 1977, *Union of South Africa* coasts into Dundee having crossed the Tay Bridge with the Pentland Round Table 'Golden Jubilee'.
G. Silcock

Right:
The late John Bellwood, Chief Mechanical Engineer of the National Railway Museum, is at the regulator as *Mallard* returns to steam at York on 28 September 1985.
Martin Sheppard

Back cover, top left:
Silver Fox was specially adorned when new in 1935, with a stainless steel fox on each side of the boiler casing. The locomotive was painted predominantly in silver grey and the bands which held the casing in position were also of stainless steel. The engine's appearance was the most striking of the four silver engines built to work the 'Silver Jubilee' streamlined train. The fittings were supplied by Samuel Fox & Co, a firm of specialist steel manufacturers at Sheffield whose trade emblem was a silver fox. The photograph was taken in April 1962 at Doncaster depot, 8 months before withdrawal.
G. W. Morrison

Back cover, bottom left:
An essential part of operating steam traction is the preparation and lubrication of the locomotive, a task the driver is carrying out on *Sir Nigel Gresley* at Carlisle Kingmoor depot, after its inaugural run in private ownership on 1 April 1967. The locomotive had received repairs and was repainted in garter blue at Crewe Works. It was an easier task for the driver to prepare an 'A4' as there was no inside valve gear to oil. The conjugated valve gear across the front of the cylinders only required periodical greasing carried out by workshop staff.
G.S. Cocks

Back cover, right:
No 60008 *Dwight D. Eisenhower* is being turned on the vacuum operated turntable at Kings Cross Top Shed in June 1963, the month the depot closed. In 1932 the 70ft diameter turntable at Top Shed had been fitted experimentally with a vacuum motor which was connected to the front of the engine by the long vacuum pipe shown. The engine was sucked round by the driver in the cab creating a brake with the vacuum ejector. The arrangement proved to be very satisfactory and was subsequently adopted for many large turntables until the end of steam.
G.S. Cocks